THE BIG BOOK OF CHRISTMAS TRIVIA

QUIZ time!

A FESTIVE QUIZ BOOK ABOUT SANTA, TRADITIONS, AND MORE

Ho, ho, ho!

Welcome to The Big Book of Christmas Trivia, where the magic of the holiday season meets the joy of testing your Christmas knowledge! Whether you're cozied up by the fire with a cup of cocoa, gathering around with family and friends, or just looking to sprinkle a little more Christmas cheer into your day, this book is packed with over 500 festive questions that will delight even the biggest holiday enthusiasts.

From Santa Claus and his merry elves to beloved holiday traditions around the world, and even the twinkling lights on your Christmas tree, you'll find something here for everyone. So, put on your favorite Christmas sweater, hum a carol or two, and dive into the fun!

Merry Christmas and let's jingle all the way to some trivia magic!

1. What is the name of the famous reindeer who leads Santa's sleigh?
a) Blitzen
b) Donner
c) Dasher
d) Rudolph

2. Where do Santa's elves live?
a) North Pole
b) South Pole
c) Greenland
d) Norway

3. What is Santa Claus also known as in some countries?
a) Father Christmas
b) Kris Kringle
c) Saint Nicholas
d) All of the above

4. What is Mrs. Claus's main role at the North Pole?
a) Toy-making
b) Helping Santa prepare for Christmas
c) Guiding the reindeer
d) Wrapping gifts

5. What do reindeer primarily eat?
a) Fish
b) Grass and lichens
c) Insects
d) Tree bark

6. What is the main job of Santa's elves?
a) Building toys
b) Training reindeer
c) Decorating Christmas trees
d) Baking cookies

7. What color is Santa's suit traditionally?
a) Green
b) Blue
c) Red
d) White

8. What is Mrs. Claus famous for baking?
a) Chocolate cake
b) Gingerbread houses
c) Sugar cookies
d) Brownies

9. What is the scientific name for reindeer?

a) Rangifer tarandus
b) Cervus elaphus
c) Bos taurus
d) Equus ferus

10. What do Santa's elves wear on their heads?

a) Crowns
b) Helmets
c) Pointy hats
d) Baseball caps

11. Where does Santa Claus live?

a) The South Pole
b) Greenland
c) North Pole
d) The Mediterranean

12. What color does Mrs. Claus usually wear?

a) Green
b) Red
c) Blue
d) White

13. Which of Santa's reindeer shares its name with a weather event?
a) Comet
b) Vixen
c) Blitzen
d) Prancer

14. How tall are most of Santa's elves described?
a) 2-3 feet
b) 6-7 feet
c) 5 feet
d) 10 inches

15. What animal pulls Santa's sleigh?
a) Horses
b) Reindeer
c) Polar bears
d) Dogs

16. Who helps Mrs. Claus in the kitchen during the holiday season?
a) The elves
b) Santa
c) The reindeer
d) Frosty the Snowman

17. Where do wild reindeer mostly live?
a) Africa
b) The Arctic
c) Australia
d) South America

18. What do elves use to check if children have been naughty or nice?
a) A magical snow globe
b) A magic mirror
c) Santa's list
d) A crystal ball

19. Which famous beverage company helped popularize Santa's red suit?
a) Pepsi
b) Coca-Cola
c) Nestle
d) Dr Pepper

20. What is Mrs. Claus's favorite winter activity?
a) Ice skating
b) Reading by the fire
c) Snowball fights
d) Decorating Christmas trees

21. True or false: Both male and female reindeer grow antlers.
a) True
b) False
c) Only in summer
d) Only at Christmas

22. Which of these jobs would you NOT see Santa's elves doing?
a) Gift wrapping
b) Sleigh repairs
c) Toy design
d) Leading the reindeer

23. What is Santa's favorite food to eat on Christmas Eve?
a) Cake
b) Candy canes
c) Cookies and milk
d) Hot cocoa

24. How does Mrs. Claus help Santa on Christmas Eve?
a) She guides the sleigh
b) She prepares his suit
c) She flies with Santa
d) She packs the reindeer food

25. What is a group of reindeer called?
a) A herd
b) A pack
c) A troop
d) A flock

26. What are the elves' favorite snacks?
a) Candy canes
b) Carrots
c) Hot dogs
d) Pizza

27. How does Santa enter homes to deliver presents?
a) Through the door
b) Through a window
c) Down the chimney
d) By teleporting

28. What is the largest artificial Christmas tree ever constructed?
a) 100 feet tall
b) 150 feet tall
c) 278 feet tall
d) 350 feet tall

29. Which color are reindeer calves usually born?
a) White
b) Gray
c) Brown
d) Golden

30. What do Santa's elves ride when they aren't working?
a) Reindeer
b) Polar bears
c) Snowmobiles
d) Sleighs

31. What does Santa Claus say when he's happy?
a) Ho Ho Ho!
b) Merry Merry!
c) Jingle Bells!
d) Tis the Season!

32. Which of these does Mrs. Claus love to drink during the winter?
a) Hot chocolate
b) Tea
c) Eggnog
d) Coffee

33. How far can a reindeer migrate in a single year?
a) 50 miles
b) 300 miles
c) 1,000 miles
d) 3,000 miles

34. What magical power do many elves have?
a) Turning invisible
b) Flying
c) Making snowstorms
d) Shrinking and growing

35. In which country did the legend of Saint Nicholas originate?
a) Italy
b) Germany
c) Turkey
d) England

36. What is the record for the largest collection of Christmas trees in one location?
a) 300 trees
b) 500 trees
c) 444 trees
d) 600 trees

37. Which reindeer is known for being the fastest?
a) Dancer
b) Vixen
c) Dasher
d) Cupid

38. What day do Santa's elves look forward to the most?
a) Christmas Eve
b) New Year's Eve
c) Santa's birthday
d) The first day of summer

39. What does Santa use to carry the presents?
a) A big bag
b) A treasure chest
c) A magic suitcase
d) A giant stocking

40. What special gift does Mrs. Claus usually give to Santa every year?
a) A new sleigh bell
b) A warm scarf
c) Homemade cookies
d) A new pair of mittens

41. How much can an adult reindeer weigh?
a) 100-150 pounds
b) 200-300 pounds
c) 400-600 pounds
d) 50-100 pounds

42. How do elves keep warm at the North Pole?
a) They wear special coats
b) They have furry boots
c) They build fires
d) They drink hot cocoa

43. What magical power does Santa's sleigh have?
a) It can fly
b) It can turn invisible
c) It can shrink
d) It moves at the speed of light

44. In which country is it traditional to eat KFC for Christmas dinner?
a) Japan
b) South Korea
c) USA
d) Brazil

45. How many reindeer typically pull Santa's sleigh (not counting Rudolph)?
a) 10
b) 12
c) 9
d) 8

46. What type of shoes do elves usually wear?
a) Boots with fur
b) Sneakers
c) Pointy shoes with bells
d) Snowshoes

47. How does Santa keep track of who is naughty or nice?
a) His elves tell him
b) Mrs. Claus keeps a list
c) He has a magical list
d) He asks the reindeer

48. What is Mrs. Claus's first name in some stories?
a) Holly
b) Mary
c) Jessica
d) Carol

49. What special ability helps reindeer travel through snow and ice?
a) They can fly
b) They have thick hooves
c) Their fur changes color
d) Their antlers can dig tunnels

50. How do elves help Santa prepare the sleigh?
a) Pack the presents
b) Feed the reindeer
c) Polish the sleigh
d) All of the above

51. Which reindeer leads Santa's sleigh?
a) Dasher
b) Blitzen
c) Comet
d) Rudolph

52. What does Mrs. Claus do when Santa is delivering presents?
a) Bakes more cookies
b) Rests by the fire
c) Keeps the elves on schedule
d) Tracks Santa's route

53. Reindeer are also known by what other name in North America?
a) Moose
b) Caribou
c) Elk
d) Deer

54. What are Santa's elves known to be experts at?
a) Making toys
b) Singing carols
c) Ice skating
d) Snowball fights

55. Which holiday does Santa deliver presents for?
a) Easter
b) Halloween
c) Christmas
d) New Year's

56. What is Mrs. Claus's favorite Christmas song?
a) Jingle Bells
b) Silent Night
c) Deck the Halls
d) Mrs. Claus Does the Mambo

57. How do reindeer noses help them in cold weather?
a) They glow red
b) They heat the air before it enters their lungs
c) They change color
d) They filter snowflakes

58. What do elves often do after Christmas?
a) Go on vacation
b) Hike through snow forests
c) Decorate Santa's house
d) Take naps

59. What is Santa Claus's favorite reindeer game?
a) Snowball fights
b) Ice skating
c) Sleigh races
d) Reindeer tag

60. What kind of workshop does Mrs. Claus help manage?
a) A toy-making workshop
b) A wrapping paper factory
c) A Christmas decoration shop
d) A candy cane factory

61. Which of Santa's reindeer shares its name with a famous Roman god?
a) Cupid
b) Vixen
c) Comet
d) Donner

62. How long have elves been working with Santa?
a) 50 years
b) 200 years
c) 500 years
d) Forever

63. Who helps Santa make toys?
a) His reindeer
b) Mrs. Claus
c) His elves
d) Frosty the Snowman

64. What is the world record for the largest number of people wrapping Christmas presents simultaneously?
a) 1,482
b) 376
c) 2,000
d) 1,682

65. What time of year do reindeer shed their antlers?
a) Summer
b) Spring
c) Winter
d) Fall

66. What musical instrument do many elves play?
a) Guitar
b) Jingle bells
c) Harmonica
d) Piano

67. What does Santa do on the day after Christmas?
a) Takes a long nap
b) Goes on vacation
c) Prepares for next year
d) Eats leftovers

68. How does Mrs. Claus stay warm in the North Pole?
a) She makes hot cocoa
b) She wears a cozy red shawl
c) She sits by the fireplace
d) All of the above

69. How fast can a reindeer run?

a) 10 miles per hour

b) 20 miles per hour

c) 50 miles per hour

d) 80 miles per hour

70. What is the name of the elf who reports back to Santa?

a) Toy Elf

b) Sleigh Master

c) Scout Elf

d) Gift Guide

71. Who checks Santa's suit to make sure it's ready for Christmas Eve?

a) The elves

b) Mrs. Claus

c) The reindeer

d) Santa himself

72. Which pet does Mrs. Claus have at the North Pole?

a) A cat

b) A polar bear

c) A penguin

d) A dog

73. What unique adaptation helps reindeer find food in the snow?
a) X-ray vision
b) Excellent sense of smell
c) Glowing eyes
d) Long tongues

74. What do elves sprinkle to make reindeer fly?
a) Fairy dust
b) Magic snow
c) Christmas cheer
d) Reindeer food

75. What color is Santa's belt?
a) Brown
b) Green
c) Red
d) Black

76. What does Mrs. Claus enjoy doing with the elves?
a) Singing Christmas carols
b) Playing board games
c) Dancing
d) Ice skating

77. What color are a reindeer's eyes during the winter months?
a) Blue
b) Brown
c) Green
d) Red

78. How do elves help Santa know what children want for Christmas?
a) They read letters to Santa
b) They guess
c) They ask the reindeer
d) They use a crystal ball

79. What does Santa do if a house doesn't have a chimney?
a) He skips it
b) He enters through a window
c) He uses magic to create a chimney
d) He leaves gifts outside

80. How does Mrs. Claus decorate the North Pole for Christmas?
a) She hangs toys
b) She makes ice sculptures
c) She plants poinsettias
d) She decorates Christmas trees

81. What do elves usually do on their breaks?
a) Ice skate
b) Watch Christmas movies
c) Have snowball fights
d) All of the above

82. How old is Santa Claus?
a) 50 years old
b) 500 years old
c) Over 1,000 years old
d) No one knows for sure

83. What holiday tradition does Mrs. Claus start every year?
a) A cookie baking contest
b) A Christmas countdown
c) Wrapping presents
d) Reindeer racing

84. Where is Santa Claus's workshop located?
a) South Pole
b) Greenland
c) The North Pole
d) Alaska

85. Which of these skills are elves very good at?
a) Cooking
b) Sewing toys
c) Carving wood
d) All of the above

86. What does Santa ride when he's not using his sleigh?
a) A magical train
b) A snowmobile
c) A flying bicycle
d) A sleigh pulled by snow dogs

87. How does Mrs. Claus keep Santa's suit clean?
a) She hand washes it
b) She sends it to the North Pole dry cleaners
c) She uses magic to clean it
d) She has the elves do it

88. What kind of climate does the North Pole have?
a) Hot and sunny
b) Dry desert
c) Cold and snowy
d) Rainy and humid

89. Where do Santa's elves do most of their work?
a) In the toy factory
b) In Santa's living room
c) In the reindeer stables
d) On Santa's sleigh

90. What does Santa use to guide his sleigh at night?
a) The stars
b) Rudolph's glowing nose
c) A magical compass
d) The moonlight

91. What holiday treat does Mrs. Claus love to make for the elves?
a) Fudge
b) Candy canes
c) Gingerbread men
d) Hot apple cider

92. Which ocean surrounds the North Pole?
a) Atlantic Ocean
b) Arctic Ocean
c) Pacific Ocean
d) Indian Ocean

93. What happens if an elf catches a cold?
a) They wear extra scarves
b) They have to rest in bed
c) Santa brings them soup
d) They get a special hot chocolate

94. What is Santa's favorite sport?
a) Snowball fights
b) Ice fishing
c) Ice skating
d) Sleigh racing

95. What book does Mrs. Claus like to read during the holiday season?
a) A Christmas Carol
b) The Night Before Christmas
c) The Nutcracker
d) The Polar Express

96. What animal is commonly found in the North Pole region?
a) Penguins
b) Polar bears
c) Kangaroos
d) Lions

97. Which of these is one of the elves' favorite holidays (besides Christmas)?
a) Thanksgiving
b) Halloween
c) Valentine's Day
d) Fourth of July

98. What country claims to be Santa's official home?
a) Canada
b) Finland
c) USA
d) Norway

99. What hobby does Mrs. Claus enjoy in her free time?
a) Painting
b) Knitting
c) Skating
d) Gardening

100. Who lives with Santa Claus at the North Pole?
a) His elves and reindeer
b) Penguins and polar bears
c) Mrs. Claus and monkeys
d) The Easter Bunny

101. Who is in charge of all the elves?
a) Head Elf
b) Mrs. Claus
c) Santa's Reindeer
d) Frosty the Snowman

102. What magical ability does Santa use to visit every house in one night?
a) Time travel
b) Flying super-fast
c) He freezes time
d) A magic sleigh route

103. How does Santa's sleigh fly over the North Pole?
a) Powered by rocket boosters
b) Pulled by magical reindeer
c) Controlled by elves
d) Floats on magic clouds

104. What country is home to the amusement park Bakken, where the World Santa Claus Congress is held?
a) Norway
b) Finland
c) Sweden
d) Denmark

105. What is the special time when elves make extra toys?
a) The Great Toy Rush
b) Santa's Crunch Time
c) Christmas Countdown
d) Toy Time

106. What makes the North Pole a magical place during Christmas?
a) The endless sunlight
b) The colorful northern lights
c) The talking animals
d) The giant Christmas tree

107. In which country is the Christmas figure "La Befana," a kind witch who brings gifts, part of the tradition?
a) Germany
b) Italy
c) Spain
d) France

108. Which country holds the record for the most Santas surfing at the same time?
a) USA
b) Australia
c) South Africa
d) Brazil

109. What do elves do if they run out of wrapping paper?
a) Make more paper from magic
b) Use blankets
c) Wrap presents in snow
d) Call Santa for help

110. What does Santa's belly do when he laughs?
a) Nothing
b) Shakes like a bowl of jelly
c) Glows
d) Shrinks

111. What special event happens every Christmas Eve at the North Pole?
a) A reindeer race
b) Santa's sleigh launch
c) Elf talent show
d) Ice skating competition

112. What is the traditional Christmas dessert called in the UK?
a) Pumpkin pie
b) Panettone
c) Christmas pudding
d) Stollen

113. What are Santa's elves always full of?
a) Christmas spirit
b) Magic snow
c) Elf juice
d) Peppermint syrup

114. Where does Santa park his sleigh when he visits homes?
a) In the driveway
b) On the street
c) On the roof
d) In the backyard

115. What do the elves at the North Pole spend most of their time doing?
a) Wrapping presents
b) Baking cookies
c) Making toys
d) Feeding the reindeer

116. Which country celebrates "Little Candles Day" to mark the start of the Christmas season?
a) Colombia
b) Argentina
c) Mexico
d) Spain

117. What do children usually leave out for Santa on Christmas Eve?

a) Cake and coffee

b) Fruit and tea

c) Cookies and milk

d) Chocolate and juice

118. How does Santa check his "Naughty and Nice" list at the North Pole?

a) By asking the elves

b) Through a magic snow globe

c) Using his magical scroll

d) By writing it down in a book

119. What is the main Christmas tree in New York City called?

a) Rockefeller Center Tree

b) Central Park Tree

c) Statue of Liberty Tree

d) Times Square Tree

120. What season does the World Santa Claus Congress take place in Denmark?

a) Winter

b) Spring

c) Summer

d) Fall

121. What is Santa's favorite weather for Christmas Eve?
a) Snowy
b) Sunny
c) Rainy
d) Windy

122. What natural phenomenon is often seen above the North Pole?
a) Solar eclipse
b) Shooting stars
c) Aurora Borealis (Northern Lights)
d) Rainbow halo

123. In which country do people celebrate Christmas with fireworks and giant lanterns?
a) China
b) The Philippines
c) Mexico
d) Thailand

124. In "It's a Wonderful Life," what is the name of the main character played by James Stewart?
a) George Bailey
b) Harry Potter
c) Clark Griswold
d) Ebenezer Scrooge

125. What type of building is Santa's workshop at the North Pole?
a) A gingerbread house
b) A wooden cabin
c) A magical ice castle
d) A cozy log cabin

126. What is the famous Christmas market in Germany called?
a) Christkindlmarkt
b) Weihnachtsdorf
c) Markt der Lichter
d) Noelmarkt

127. In the movie "Home Alone," where does Kevin's family go for Christmas vacation?
a) Paris
b) New York
c) London
d) Hawaii

128. Since which year has the World Santa Claus Congress been held annually in Denmark?
a) 1947
b) 1957
c) 1967
d) 1977

129. How does Santa keep track of Christmas wishes?
a) His elves listen to kids
b) He reads letters
c) He uses a magic snow globe
d) Mrs. Claus tells him

130. What time of year is it dark all day at the North Pole?
a) Spring
b) Summer
c) Fall
d) Winter

131. In which country do children receive gifts from "Jultomten," a Christmas gnome?
a) Denmark
b) Finland
c) Sweden
d) Iceland

132. What does Buddy the Elf use to decorate the Christmas tree in "Elf"?
a) Candy
b) Popcorn
c) Ribbons
d) Glitter

133. Which holiday does Santa prepare for all year?
a) Halloween
b) Thanksgiving
c) Christmas
d) New Year's Eve

134. What do the reindeer eat to stay strong and healthy at the North Pole?
a) Ice cream
b) Candy canes
c) Magical oats
d) Hot chocolate

135. Which country is famous for its tradition of hiding brooms on Christmas Eve to prevent witches from stealing them?
a) Norway
b) Russia
c) Poland
d) Hungary

136. In "A Christmas Carol," who visits Ebenezer Scrooge on Christmas Eve?
a) The Ghost of Christmas Present
b) The Ghost of Christmas Past
c) The Ghost of Christmas Yet to Come
d) All of the above

137. What sound do Santa's reindeer make when they land on the roof?
a) Thump thump
b) Jingle jingle
c) Clip clop
d) Swish swoosh

138. Which famous animal can only be found in the Arctic, near the North Pole?
a) Koala
b) Polar bear
c) Camel
d) Sloth

139. Which country celebrates "Las Posadas," a reenactment of Mary and Joseph's search for shelter?
a) Mexico
b) Guatemala
c) Argentina
d) Ecuador

140. In which amusement park does the World Santa Claus Congress take place every year?
a) Tivoli Gardens
b) Bakken
c) Efteling
d) Disneyland Paris

141. Where does Santa's magic sleigh take off from on Christmas Eve?
a) His workshop
b) A giant ice runway
c) The roof of his house
d) The North Pole sleighport

142. What is Mrs. Claus's favorite thing to do at the North Pole?
a) Ice skating
b) Baking cookies
c) Feeding the reindeer
d) Decorating the workshop

143. In which country do people exchange gifts on "Boxing Day" (December 26)?
a) Australia
b) Canada
c) United Kingdom
d) All of the above

144. What is the world record for the most expensive Christmas tree ever decorated?
a) $1.2 million
b) $11 million
c) $15 million
d) $500,000

145. How do Santa's elves help Santa on Christmas Eve?
a) They guide the reindeer
b) They pack the presents in the sleigh
c) They keep track of the children's lists
d) They take care of Mrs. Claus

146. How does Santa stay warm at the North Pole?
a) By drinking hot cocoa
b) Wearing his red suit and boots
c) By sitting near the fire
d) All of the above

147. In what country is the Christmas Eve feast called "Réveillon"?
a) France
b) Belgium
c) Switzerland
d) Canada

148. In "The Polar Express," what is the first gift of Christmas?
a) A bell
b) A toy train
c) A gold star
d) A Christmas tree

149. What does Santa say when he leaves a house after delivering gifts?
a) Merry Christmas to all, and to all a good night!
b) Ho Ho Ho, see you next year!
c) I'll be back!
d) Happy Holidays!

150. How do the reindeer practice for Christmas Eve at the North Pole?
a) They pull Santa's sleigh around the North Pole
b) They go on training flights
c) They play reindeer games
d) They run laps around the workshop

151. Which country is known for its Christmas tradition of "Carols by Candlelight"?
a) Australia
b) USA
c) South Africa
d) Canada

152. In the animated movie "How the Grinch Stole Christmas," what is the Grinch's dog's name?
a) Max
b) Rufus
c) Charlie
d) Gizmo

153. Who helps Santa deliver presents to children around the world?
a) His elves
b) His reindeer
c) Mrs. Claus
d) All of the above

154. What special celebration do the elves have at the North Pole after Christmas?
a) Elf Appreciation Day
b) Reindeer Olympics
c) Hot Chocolate Party
d) Snowball Tournament

155. In which country do children put shoes by the fireplace for Santa to fill?
a) France
b) Belgium
c) Germany
d) The Netherlands

156. Which Christmas movie features a boy who learns the true meaning of Christmas after being visited by three spirits?
a) A Christmas Story
b) Miracle on 34th Street
c) A Christmas Carol
d) The Santa Clause

157. What does Santa love to read even when he's not working?
a) Christmas carol lyrics
b) Children's letters
c) Books about reindeer
d) His toy-making manual

158. What special star shines over the North Pole on Christmas Eve?
a) The North Star
b) The Star of Bethlehem
c) The Midnight Star
d) The Santa Star

159. What is the Christmas character "Krampus" known for in Austria?
a) Bringing coal to parents
b) Scaring bad children
c) Delivering presents
d) Helping Santa pack his sleigh

160. In "A Christmas Story," what gift does Ralphie desperately want for Christmas?
a) A toy train
b) A BB gun
c) A bicycle
d) A puppy

161. What holiday tradition do the elves enjoy at the North Pole?
a) Making snow angels
b) Decorating the workshop
c) Singing Christmas carols
d) All of the above

162. In what country is it traditional to have a barbecue on Christmas Day?
a) New Zealand
b) Brazil
c) Australia
d) South Africa

163. What is the name of the department store in "Miracle on 34th Street"?
a) Macy's
b) Bloomingdale's
c) Gimbels
d) Sears

164. What is the record for the largest gathering of people dressed as Santa Claus?
a) 10,000
b) 13,000
c) 18,112
d) 4,256

**165. Which country has a tradition called
"Jolabokaflod," where people give books on
Christmas Eve?**
a) Finland
b) Norway
c) Iceland
d) Denmark

**166. What song does Bing Crosby sing in "White
Christmas"?**
a) Jingle Bells
b) I'm Dreaming of a White Christmas
c) Silent Night
d) Deck the Halls

**167. What is the best-selling Christmas song of all
time?**
a) Last Christmas
b) White Christmas
c) Jingle Bells
d) Rudolph the Red-Nosed Reindeer

**168. In what year did the Rockefeller Center
Christmas Tree lighting ceremony begin?**
a) 1920
b) 1933
c) 1945
d) 1950

169. How do Santa's letters from children get to the North Pole?
a) By magic mailboxes
b) Through a secret tunnel
c) The reindeer deliver them
d) Santa picks them up on his sleigh

170. Which country celebrates "Sinterklaas" instead of Santa Claus?
a) The Netherlands
b) Belgium
c) Spain
d) Italy

171. In "The Nightmare Before Christmas," who is the King of Halloween Town?
a) Jack Skellington
b) Oogie Boogie
c) Sally
d) Santa Claus

172. In the song "Jingle Bells," what is pulled by the horse?
a) A sleigh
b) A wagon
c) A car
d) A carriage

173. What do the Northern Lights look like above the North Pole?
a) Bright white snowflakes
b) Colorful dancing lights
c) Golden stars
d) Floating clouds

174. In which country is Christmas celebrated with a festive meal called "Nochebuena"?
a) Spain
b) Canada
c) Portugal
d) India

175. What is the name of the little girl in "The Santa Clause"?
a) Lucy
b) Judy
c) Claire
d) Mary

176. Which Christmas carol features the line "Fa la la la la, la la la la"?
a) Joy to the World
b) Deck the Halls
c) Hark! The Herald Angels Sing
d) O Holy Night

177. How long does it take Santa to fly from the North Pole to every home on Christmas Eve?
a) All night
b) A few days
c) Only a few hours
d) Just one second

178. In what country is Santa known as "Father Frost" or "Ded Moroz"?
a) Russia
b) Ukraine
c) Belarus
d) All of the above

179. In "Rudolph the Red-Nosed Reindeer," who is Rudolph's elf friend?
a) Hermey
b) Clarice
c) Yukon Cornelius
d) Santa Claus

180. What does the singer in "Frosty the Snowman" do when he comes to life?
a) He dances
b) He runs away
c) He laughs
d) He sings

181. How do the elves stay entertained at the North Pole when they're not working?
a) They watch Christmas movies
b) They play in the snow
c) They have reindeer races
d) All of the above

182. What is the name of the traditional Christmas drink in Puerto Rico?
a) Hot chocolate
b) Eggnog
c) Coquito
d) Ponche

183. In "Christmas Vacation," what does Clark Griswold want to buy with his Christmas bonus?
a) A new car
b) A swimming pool
c) A big-screen TV
d) A vacation

184. Where was the world's largest Christmas cake made?
a) Japan
b) Canada
c) Italy
d) India

185. What do the North Pole elves wear to stay warm?
a) Christmas sweaters
b) Santa suits
c) Colorful coats and hats
d) T-shirts

186. In which country is it common to eat "Panettone" during Christmas?
a) Italy
b) France
c) Spain
d) Germany

187. What does Frosty the Snowman come to life with?
a) A magic wand
b) A top hat
c) A scarf
d) A pair of gloves

188. In the song "Rudolph the Red-Nosed Reindeer," what does Rudolph guide?
a) Santa's sleigh
b) A Christmas tree
c) A reindeer caravan
d) Mrs. Claus

189. What magical feature does Santa's sleigh have?
a) It can fly faster than light
b) It can turn invisible
c) It shrinks to fit into small spaces
d) All of the above

190. Which country celebrates Christmas with "Vigilia," a fish dinner on Christmas Eve?
a) Poland
b) Greece
c) Italy
d) Slovakia

191. In "The Muppet Christmas Carol," who plays Ebenezer Scrooge?
a) Kermit the Frog
b) Michael Caine
c) Gonzo
d) Fozzie Bear

192. What is the longest Yule log ever baked?
a) 1,000 feet
b) 2,000 feet
c) 300 feet
d) 1,069 feet

193. What is the only way to reach Santa's workshop at the North Pole?
a) By flying with reindeer
b) Walking through the snow
c) Riding a magical train
d) By snowmobile

194. In what country is Christmas celebrated by eating "tamales"?
a) Mexico
b) Argentina
c) Colombia
d) Brazil

195. What gift does Santa give to the children in "The Santa Clause"?
a) A puppy
b) Toys
c) A sleigh ride
d) A snowman

196. What type of tree is mentioned in "O Christmas Tree"?
a) Pine
b) Spruce
c) Fir
d) Oak

**197. Which country has the tradition of "Caga Tió,"
a Christmas log that "poops" presents?**
a) Spain
b) Portugal
c) Italy
d) Greece

**198. In "Jingle All the Way," what toy does Howard
Langston desperately try to find for his son?**
a) Tickle Me Elmo
b) Turbo Man
c) Buzz Lightyear
d) Power Ranger

**199. In which popular Christmas song the narrator
says that it's better to watch out, not cry?**
a) Santa Claus Is Coming to Town
b) Jingle Bell Rock
c) Frosty the Snowman
d) We Wish You a Merry Christmas

**200. What is the main purpose of Santa's
workshop?**
a) Making toys
b) Wrapping presents
c) Baking cookies
d) Organizing the naughty and nice list

201. In which country do people attend a "Misa de Gallo," or "Rooster's Mass" on Christmas Eve?
a) Philippines
b) Portugal
c) Romania
d) Poland

202. What is the main theme of the song "The Twelve Days of Christmas"?
a) A journey
b) Gift-giving
c) Family gatherings
d) Winter celebrations

203. In what year did "Elf," starring Will Ferrell, first hit theaters?
a) 2000
b) 2003
c) 2005
d) 2007

204. In what year did Queen Elizabeth II give her first televised Christmas message?
a) 1957
b) 1965
c) 1970
d) 1950

205. What is the traditional Christmas food eaten in Japan?
a) Sushi
b) Fried chicken
c) Ramen
d) Tempura

206. In "The Holiday," which two actresses star as the main characters who swap homes for Christmas?
a) Cameron Diaz and Kate Winslet
b) Reese Witherspoon and Jennifer Aniston
c) Drew Barrymore and Sandra Bullock
d) Anne Hathaway and Meryl Streep

207. Who wrote the famous Christmas song "Silent Night"?
a) Franz Gruber
b) J.S. Bach
c) Irving Berlin
d) Nat King Cole

208. In Santa's workshop, who typically operates the sewing machines?
a) Santa
b) Elves
c) Reindeer
d) Mrs. Claus

209. Which country has a Christmas tradition of "Gävle Goat," a giant straw goat?
a) Sweden
b) Norway
c) Finland
d) Denmark

210. Which Christmas movie features a man who becomes Santa Claus after an accident?
a) The Santa Clause
b) Miracle on 34th Street
c) Elf
d) Frosty Returns

211. In "We Wish You a Merry Christmas," what do the singers demand?
a) A carol
b) A drink
c) A gift
d) A cookie

212. What kind of machinery might be found in Santa's workshop for assembling toys?
a) Lathes
b) Printers
c) Excavators
d) Mixers

213. Which African country celebrates Christmas on January 7, according to the Orthodox calendar?
a) Kenya
b) Ethiopia
c) Nigeria
d) Ghana

214. In which song does the narrator dream of a white Christmas?
a) Have Yourself a Merry Little Christmas
b) Winter Wonderland
c) White Christmas
d) Let It Snow

215. Which tool would Santa use for wrapping gifts?
a) Tape dispenser
b) Glue gun
c) Paintbrush
d) Drill

216. What is the world record for the most lights lit on a Christmas tree?
a) 500,000
b) 194,672
c) 745,000
d) 250,000

**217. What do people in Finland often do on
Christmas Eve?**

a) Visit a sauna

b) Bake cookies

c) Go skiing

d) Watch a Christmas movie

**218. In "Home Alone 2," where does Kevin find
himself after getting separated from his family?**

a) Chicago

b) New York City

c) Los Angeles

d) Miami

**219. What does the narrator ask Santa to bring in
the song "Santa Baby"?**

a) A yacht

b) A diamond ring

c) A new car

d) A puppy

**220. What is the primary material that Santa's elves
use to make plush toys?**

a) Wood

b) Metal

c) Fabric

d) Plastic

221. In what country do people eat "Stollen" as a traditional Christmas dessert?
a) Germany
b) Austria
c) Switzerland
d) Belgium

222. Which animated Christmas movie features a train that takes children to the North Pole?
a) The Polar Express
b) Arthur Christmas
c) Elf
d) The Grinch

223. In "Hark! The Herald Angels Sing," what do the angels proclaim?
a) Peace on Earth
b) Joy to the World
c) Glory to the Newborn King
d) Joy to the Angels

224. What do Santa's elves use to decorate toys?
a) Markers
b) Glitter and paint
c) Stickers
d) All of the above

225. Which country is known for its "Feast of the Seven Fishes" on Christmas Eve?
a) Italy
b) Spain
c) Portugal
d) Croatia

226. What does the character Buddy famously declare about syrup in "Elf"?
a) It's a topping for pancakes
b) It's great on spaghetti
c) It's a dessert
d) It's a drink

227. What type of vehicle do Santa's elves use to transport toys around the workshop?
a) Sleigh
b) Elf carts
c) Reindeer
d) Trains

228. In what year was the song "Do They Know It's Christmas?" by Band Aid released?
a) 1979
b) 1984
c) 1990
d) 1995

229. What country has a tradition of eating oysters for Christmas?
a) France
b) Italy
c) Japan
d) Brazil

230. In "A Christmas Carol," who is Scrooge's underpaid clerk?
a) Bob Cratchit
b) Tiny Tim
c) Jacob Marley
d) Fred

231. Which tool would be essential for making toy cars?
a) Pliers
b) Ruler
c) Sandpaper
d) All of the above

232. Where was the world's largest nativity scene created, with over 800 figures?
a) Spain
b) Mexico
c) Italy
d) USA

233. In which country do people celebrate Christmas with the "Star of Bethlehem" ceremony?
a) Poland
b) Israel
c) Greece
d) Romania

234. In "Miracle on 34th Street," who plays the role of Kris Kringle?
a) Edmund Gwenn
b) Tom Hanks
c) Richard Attenborough
d) John Goodman

235. What traditional song is sung by carolers who are asking for food and drink?
a) We Wish You a Merry Christmas
b) God Rest Ye Merry, Gentlemen
c) Good King Wenceslas
d) O Come, O Come, Emmanuel

236. What do elves use to create magical snowflakes for decorations?
a) Magic wand
b) Snow machine
c) Paper and scissors
d) Glue and glitter

237. Which country has a tradition of "Santons,"
small Christmas figurines in a nativity scene?
a) France
b) Spain
c) Belgium
d) Italy

238. In "The Nightmare Before Christmas," what
holiday does Jack Skellington try to take over?
a) Halloween
b) Thanksgiving
c) Easter
d) Valentine's Day

239. What do the lyrics of "Jingle Bell Rock"
mention?
a) Snowflakes
b) A rock and roll party
c) Christmas trees
d) A sleigh ride

240. In what year did the film "The Polar Express"
release?
a) 2000
b) 2002
c) 2004
d) 2006

241. In what country do people celebrate Christmas with a cake shaped like a log called "Bûche de Noël"?
a) France
b) Italy
c) Germany
d) Switzerland

242. What does the Grinch hate the most about Christmas?
a) The gifts
b) The decorations
c) The noise
d) The food

243. What kind of machine do elves use to wrap gifts quickly?
a) Gift-wrapping machine
b) Sewing machine
c) Conveyor belt
d) Packing machine

244. What is the most popular type of Christmas tree in the United States?
a) Douglas Fir
b) Noble Fir
c) Frasier Fir
d) Balsam Fir

245. Which country celebrates "Jul," a midwinter festival similar to Christmas?
a) Sweden
b) Iceland
c) Norway
d) Finland

246. What tool do elves use to assemble model kits?
a) Screwdriver
b) Wrench
c) Hammer
d) Needle

247. What do elves use to create colorful gift tags?
a) Printer
b) Scissors and markers
c) Paper cutter
d) All of the above

248. What is traditionally placed at the top of a Christmas tree?
a) A star
b) An angel
c) A bow
d) A bell

249. In what country is Christmas associated with the tradition of eating a meat pie called "Tourtière"?
a) Canada
b) France
c) Australia
d) Spain

250. What magical item helps Santa to know if children are naughty or nice?
a) Crystal ball
b) Naughty/Nice List
c) Elf communicator
d) Magic mirror

251. What do the elves use to ensure toys are safe for children?
a) Quality control checklist
b) Magic wand
c) Test children
d) Labeling machine

252. Which country is credited with starting the Christmas tree tradition?
a) United States
b) Germany
c) France
d) England

253. Which country celebrates Christmas with a character called "Père Noël"?
a) France
b) Belgium
c) Luxembourg
d) All of the above

254. Which tool would Santa use to measure toy dimensions accurately?
a) Protractor
b) Measuring tape
c) Caliper
d) Ruler

255. What type of tool do elves use for carving intricate designs into toys?
a) Knife
b) Lathe
c) Dremel
d) All of the above

256. What is the traditional color of Christmas tree lights?
a) Blue
b) Red
c) White
d) Multicolored

257. What is Santa's favorite tool for putting the finishing touches on toys?

a) Paintbrush

b) Glue stick

c) Magic wand

d) Spray can

258. What year was the first electric Christmas tree light set invented?

a) 1882

b) 1901

c) 1920

d) 1945

259. Which popular Christmas carol mentions a "Christmas tree"?

a) O Christmas Tree

b) Jingle Bells

c) Silent Night

d) Frosty the Snowman

260. What event is celebrated on Christmas Day in the Christian tradition?

a) The Resurrection of Jesus

b) The birth of Jesus Christ

c) The Ascension of Jesus

d) The Last Supper

261. What is the purpose of a Christmas tree stand?
a) Decoration
b) Support
c) Storage
d) None of the above

262. What do many people use to decorate their Christmas trees?
a) Flowers
b) Ribbons
c) Ornaments
d) All of the above

263. What is a common tradition involving Christmas trees in many households?
a) Burning them after Christmas
b) Hanging stockings on them
c) Decorating them with family
d) Leaving them outside

264. Who was the mother of Jesus?
a) Mary
b) Elizabeth
c) Sarah
d) Martha

265. What is the name of the traditional Christmas tree ornament that resembles a glass bauble?
a) Tinsel
b) Bulb
c) Bauble
d) Star

266. Which U.S. state is the largest producer of Christmas trees?
a) Oregon
b) North Carolina
c) Michigan
d) Pennsylvania

267. Which figure is known for his role as the earthly father of Jesus?
a) Joseph
b) Peter
c) John
d) Andrew

268. In what year was the famous poem "A Visit from St. Nicholas" (Twas the Night Before Christmas) first published?
a) 1789
b) 1812
c) 1823
d) 1850

269. What natural feature do people often use to scent their Christmas trees?
a) Pine needles
b) Cinnamon sticks
c) Peppermint
d) Cloves

270. What is often placed underneath a Christmas tree?
a) Snow
b) Presents
c) Ornaments
d) Lights

271. What city is traditionally recognized as the birthplace of Jesus?
a) Nazareth
b) Jerusalem
c) Bethlehem
d) Galilee

272. In what year did the movie "Home Alone" premiere in theaters?
a) 1989
b) 1990
c) 1993
d) 1995

273. How tall can the tallest Christmas trees grow?
a) 5 feet
b) 10 feet
c) 15 feet
d) Over 100 feet

274. What do people often do to prevent their Christmas trees from drying out?
a) Water them regularly
b) Spray them with oil
c) Use artificial snow
d) Place them in a corner

275. What is the traditional time frame for putting up a Christmas tree?
a) After Halloween
b) The day after Thanksgiving
c) On Christmas Eve
d) After New Year's

276. In the nativity story, who announced the birth of Jesus to the shepherds?
a) The Wise Men
b) Mary
c) Angels
d) Joseph

277. **What is a common way to dispose of a Christmas tree after the holiday season?**
a) Burning
b) Recycling
c) Throwing it away
d) Giving it to friends

278. **What is the significance of the Christmas tree in Christmas celebrations?**
a) It symbolizes winter
b) It represents family gatherings
c) It signifies life and renewal
d) It is a decoration only

279. **What is the significance of the manger in the Christmas story?**
a) It was a place for animals
b) It symbolizes humility
c) It represents shelter
d) All of the above

280. **In what year did Coca-Cola first feature Santa Claus in their holiday advertisements?**
a) 1925
b) 1931
c) 1945
d) 1950

281. What do many people place in their homes to celebrate the Christmas story?
a) A Christmas tree
b) A nativity scene
c) Advent wreaths
d) All of the above

282. What gifts were brought by the Wise Men to honor baby Jesus?
a) Gold, frankincense, and myrrh
b) Silver and jewels
c) Food and clothing
d) Toys and games

283. What role does the story of Jesus' birth play in the broader context of hope and peace during the holiday season?
a) It is a reminder of new beginnings
b) It emphasizes the importance of family
c) It inspires acts of kindness and charity
d) All of the above

284. In what year was the song "All I Want for Christmas Is You" by Mariah Carey released?
a) 1991
b) 1994
c) 1996
d) 2000

285. What is the most popular candy cane flavor?
a) Peppermint
b) Cinnamon
c) Chocolate
d) Cherry

286. Which of these is not a traditional Christmas cookie?
a) Gingerbread
b) Sugar cookie
c) Whoopie pie
d) Oatmeal raisin cookie

287. What is the main ingredient in panettone?
a) Chocolate
b) Fruit
c) Nuts
d) Bread

288. What is the name of the traditional French Christmas log cake?
a) Bûche de Noël
b) Yule Log
c) Christmas Cake
d) Panettone

289. What is an ingredient in eggnog?
a) Milk
b) Eggs
c) Cream
d) All of the above

290. Which of these is not a traditional Christmas cocktail?
a) Mulled wine
b) Hot toddy
c) Margarita
d) Wassail

291. Which of these is a traditional Christmas punch?
a) Sangria
b) Apple cider
c) Wassail
d) All of the above

292. In what year was the TV special "Rudolph the Red-Nosed Reindeer" first aired?
a) 1958
b) 1964
c) 1971
d) 1980

293. What is the name of the candy often associated with Christmas stockings?
a) Reese's Pieces
b) M&Ms
c) Peeps
d) Candy canes

294. What is the main ingredient in marzipan?
a) Sugar
b) Almonds
c) Chocolate
d) Nuts

295. What is the name of the Christmas-themed popcorn snack often covered in caramel and chocolate?
a) Kettle corn
b) Crackerjack
c) Christmas Crunch
d) Popcorn balls

296. What is the name of the traditional Italian Christmas pastry filled with ricotta cheese and candied fruit?
a) Panforte
b) Cannoli
c) Tiramisu
d) Zeppole

297. What is the name of the Scandinavian Christmas drink made with spiced wine and almonds?
a) Glögg
b) Wassail
c) Mulled wine
d) Hot toddy

298. What is the main ingredient in hot toddy?
a) Whiskey
b) Rum
c) Vodka
d) Tequila

299. Which of these is not a traditional ingredient in mulled wine?
a) Cinnamon
b) Orange slices
c) Lemon juice
d) Coconut

300. What is the name of the traditional Christmas punch made with cider, brandy, and spices?
a) Wassail
b) Sangria
c) Punch bowl
d) Hot toddy

301. What is the name of the traditional Mexican Christmas drink made with hot chocolate, cinnamon, and chili peppers?
a) Champurrado
b) Horchata
c) Atole
d) Ponche

302. In which century did Christmas begin to be widely celebrated as a Christian holiday?
a) 1st century
b) 4th century
c) 8th century
d) 12th century

303. Which Roman festival influenced many of the traditions associated with Christmas?
a) Saturnalia
b) Lupercalia
c) Bacchanalia
d) Floralia

304. When was December 25th officially declared as the date for Christmas by the Roman Church?
a) 202 AD
b) 312 AD
c) 336 AD
d) 450 AD

305. What was Christmas originally called in England before being known by its current name?
a) Yuletide
b) Winter Feast
c) Christ's Mass
d) Midwinter Festival

306. Which Puritan leader banned the celebration of Christmas in England during the 17th century?
a) Oliver Cromwell
b) King Charles I
c) William Laud
d) Thomas Fairfax

307. In what century did Christmas become a public holiday in the United States?
a) 17th century
b) 18th century
c) 19th century
d) 20th century

308. Which famous book by Charles Dickens greatly influenced the modern Christmas celebration?
a) Great Expectations
b) Oliver Twist
c) A Christmas Carol
d) David Copperfield

309. Which ancient culture's winter solstice celebration shares some similarities with modern Christmas traditions?
a) Greek
b) Egyptian
c) Norse
d) Celtic

310. Which U.S. state was the first to recognize Christmas as an official holiday?
a) New York
b) Virginia
c) Alabama
d) Massachusetts

311. What did the Puritans in colonial America think about Christmas celebrations?
a) They encouraged them
b) They celebrated quietly
c) They banned them
d) They had no opinion

312. Who introduced the idea of Santa Claus to America in the 19th century?
a) Dutch settlers
b) English colonists
c) French traders
d) Italian immigrants

313. The Christmas carol "Silent Night" was composed in which country?

a) Austria

b) Germany

c) Switzerland

d) France

314. In medieval times, what was commonly eaten at Christmas feasts in Europe?

a) Roast turkey

b) Goose

c) Ham

d) Venison

315. When did the Christmas card tradition begin?

a) 1770s

b) 1820s

c) 1840s

d) 1900s

316. What was the original name of the "Yule log" tradition, which is now part of Christmas?

a) Winter Log

b) Hearth Log

c) Yuletide Fire

d) Christmas Block

317. Which British monarch popularized the Christmas tree in the 19th century?
a) Queen Victoria
b) King George III
c) Queen Elizabeth I
d) King Edward VII

318. What pagan festival influenced early Christmas celebrations in Scandinavian countries?
a) Yule
b) Valborg
c) Samhain
d) Beltane

319. Which modern Christmas tradition was brought to the U.S. by German immigrants?
a) Hanging stockings
b) The Christmas tree
c) Decorating with holly
d) The Yule log

320. Which country is believed to have sent the first official Christmas cards?
a) England
b) France
c) Germany
d) Italy

321. Which dessert is commonly associated with Christmas in England?
a) Cheesecake
b) Christmas pudding
c) Apple pie
d) Shortbread

322. What alcoholic beverage is often served warm during Christmas?
a) Mulled wine
b) Eggnog
c) Hot buttered rum
d) Irish coffee

323. What popular Christmas cookie is shaped like little men?
a) Sugar cookies
b) Gingerbread cookies
c) Shortbread
d) Chocolate chip cookies

324. What holiday TV special features a boy trying to get a Red Ryder BB gun?
a) It's a Wonderful Life
b) A Christmas Story
c) Miracle on 34th Street
d) Home Alone

325. What Christmas beverage is traditionally made with milk, sugar, cream, and beaten eggs?
a) Eggnog
b) Hot chocolate
c) Wassail
d) Cider

326. What is a popular spice often added to Christmas cookies and drinks?
a) Nutmeg
b) Cumin
c) Cayenne
d) Oregano

327. Which fruit is commonly associated with Christmas fruitcake?
a) Apples
b) Strawberries
c) Dried fruits
d) Bananas

328. In Italy, what sweet bread is traditionally served during Christmas?
a) Panettone
b) Brioche
c) Croissant
d) Baguette

329. Which hot beverage is often enjoyed by the fire during the holiday season?
a) Hot cocoa
b) Green tea
c) Lemonade
d) Black coffee

330. What ingredient is typically used to make peppermint bark?
a) White chocolate and peppermint
b) Milk chocolate and cinnamon
c) Dark chocolate and almonds
d) Vanilla and caramel

331. What traditional Christmas beverage originates from Scandinavian countries?
a) Glögg
b) Cider
c) Sangria
d) Limoncello

332. In "A Garfield Christmas Special," what does Jon's grandmother give Garfield for Christmas?
a) A new bed
b) A book of poems
c) Lasagna
d) A back scratch

333. What is often added to eggnog to make it a festive adult beverage?
a) Whiskey
b) Rum
c) Vodka
d) Brandy

334. Which type of pie is often associated with Christmas in the United States?
a) Pumpkin pie
b) Pecan pie
c) Apple pie
d) Mince pie

335. Which dried fruit is commonly used in Christmas pudding?
a) Raisins
b) Apricots
c) Bananas
d) Pineapple

336. What is the key ingredient in a traditional Yule log cake?
a) Biscuit dough
b) Chocolate
c) Almonds
d) Vanilla cream

337. Which nut is often roasted as a Christmas treat, as mentioned in a popular Christmas song?
a) Walnuts
b) Almonds
c) Chestnuts
d) Hazelnuts

338. What is the name of the spiced drink often associated with Christmas markets in Germany?
a) Mulled cider
b) Eggnog
c) Glühwein
d) Spiced tea

339. Which traditional dessert is made with layers of sponge cake and custard, often served during Christmas in the UK?
a) Tiramisu
b) Trifle
c) Cheesecake
d) Panna cotta

340. In the song "The Twelve Days of Christmas," how many total gifts are given?
a) 78
b) 144
c) 364
d) 432

341. What is Frosty the Snowman's nose made of?

a) Carrot

b) Button

c) Rock

d) Coal

342. What is the highest-grossing Christmas movie of all time?

a) Home Alone

b) Elf

c) The Grinch (2018)

d) The Polar Express

343. What reindeer is never mentioned in "The Night Before Christmas"?

a) Dasher

b) Rudolph

c) Comet

d) Dancer

344. In which country do they say "Feliz Navidad" to wish someone a Merry Christmas?

a) Italy

b) Spain

c) France

d) Portugal

345. Which country is the largest exporter of Christmas trees?

a) United States

b) Norway

c) Canada

d) Germany

346. What is the name of the fruitcake-like Christmas bread traditionally eaten in Germany?

a) Panettone

b) Stollen

c) Baguette

d) Brioche

347. Which country donates the Christmas tree to be placed in London's Trafalgar Square each year?

a) Sweden

b) Norway

c) Finland

d) Denmark

348. What is Santa Claus called in France?

a) Father Frost

b) Père Noël

c) Santa Klaus

d) Saint Nick

349. How many ghosts are there in A Christmas Carol?

a) 1

b) 2

c) 3

d) 4

350. What decoration do you commonly find on top of a Christmas tree?

a) Star

b) Snowflake

c) Angel

d) All of the above

351. In The Polar Express, what word does the conductor punch into the main character's train ticket?

a) Believe

b) Magic

c) Faith

d) Hope

352. What does Santa traditionally leave in the stockings of children who misbehave?

a) Rocks

b) Coal

c) Sticks

d) Old candy

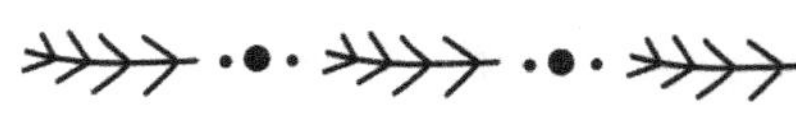

353. How many points does a snowflake traditionally have?
a) 4
b) 6
c) 8
d) 5

354. What popular toy fad was originally a Christmas gift in the 1990s?
a) Tamagotchi
b) Beanie Babies
c) Furby
d) Tickle Me Elmo

355. In what country did eggnog originate?
a) France
b) United States
c) England
d) Canada

356. What is the record for the most Christmas crackers pulled simultaneously?
a) 1,200
b) 2,000
c) 1,478
d) 2,900

357. Which Christmas tradition involves people kissing under a plant?
a) Holly
b) Ivy
c) Poinsettia
d) Mistletoe

358. Which Christmas-themed ballet premiered in 1892?
a) Swan Lake
b) The Nutcracker
c) Sleeping Beauty
d) The Firebird

359. How long does it take a tree to grow to an average Christmas tree height of 6-7 feet?
a) 5 years
b) 10 years
c) 15 years
d) 20 years

360. What color are the berries of mistletoe?
a) Red
b) White
c) Blue
d) Green

361. What famous Christmas song was written by Irving Berlin?
a) "Jingle Bells"
b) "White Christmas"
c) "Winter Wonderland"
d) "Silent Night"

362. Which Christmas song contains the lyric "I don't want a lot for Christmas"?
a) "Jingle Bell Rock"
b) "Santa Baby"
c) "All I Want for Christmas Is You"
d) "Last Christmas"

363. Which holiday was The Nightmare Before Christmas originally released for?
a) Halloween
b) Thanksgiving
c) Christmas
d) New Year's Eve

364. Which Christmas decoration was originally made from silver?
a) Tinsel
b) Ornaments
c) Ribbons
d) Wreaths

365. Which holiday plant is often used as a symbol for peace and love during Christmas?
a) Holly
b) Mistletoe
c) Ivy
d) Poinsettia

366. What Christmas tradition involves hanging socks or stockings by the fireplace?
a) Stocking stuffing
b) Yule log
c) Ornament decorating
d) Tree lighting

367. What is the name of the log burned during the 12 days of Christmas in some European countries?
a) Yule log
b) Hearth log
c) Firewood log
d) Noel log

368. What do people traditionally place under the Christmas tree for good luck?
a) A pine cone
b) A coin
c) A gift
d) A candy cane

369. In which country is a "Christmas cracker" a popular festive item?
a) United States
b) Australia
c) United Kingdom
d) Canada

370. What is the significance of the Advent calendar in the Christmas tradition?
a) To count down the days until New Year's
b) To count down the days until Christmas
c) To celebrate Santa Claus
d) To remember the 12 days of Christmas

371. In "Mickey's Christmas Carol," which character plays the role of Ebenezer Scrooge?
a) Mickey Mouse
b) Donald Duck
c) Scrooge McDuck
d) Goofy

372. The world's tallest living Christmas tree is located in which U.S. state?
a) Oregon
b) California
c) Washington
d) New York

373. Which country is known for the custom of lighting candles on the graves of loved ones on Christmas Eve?
a) Norway
b) Sweden
c) Finland
d) Iceland

374. What is the name of the Icelandic tradition where people exchange books on Christmas Eve?
a) Book Night
b) Yule Book Flood
c) Christmas Book Fair
d) Midnight Storytelling

375. In which country do children leave their shoes out to be filled with candy on St. Nicholas Day?
a) Netherlands
b) Belgium
c) Germany
d) All of the above

376. What is the record for the largest display of Christmas lights on a tree?
a) 194,672 lights
b) 151,000 lights
c) 50,000 lights
d) 100,000 lights

377. What do people in Sweden call the giant Christmas goat erected yearly in Gävle?
a) Yule Goat
b) Christmas Deer
c) Festive Elk
d) Holiday Moose

378. What day is known as Boxing Day, celebrated in the UK and some Commonwealth nations?
a) December 23
b) December 24
c) December 26
d) January 1

379. Which tradition involves a large star-shaped lantern carried in processions in the Philippines during Christmas?
a) Simbang Gabi
b) Pasko
c) Parol
d) Kutsinta

380. What is the record for the largest collection of Santa Claus memorabilia?
a) 6,278 items
b) 10,236 items
c) 4,605 items
d) 8,000 items

381. In Catalonia, what is the unusual Christmas tradition involving a log that defecates presents?
a) Caganer
b) Tió de Nadal
c) Fum, Fum, Fum
d) La Befana

382. In which country is Christmas known as "Weihnachten"?
a) Germany
b) Austria
c) Switzerland
d) All of the above

383. Which animal pulls Santa's sleigh in Australia, according to local tradition?
a) Kangaroos
b) Horses
c) Camels
d) Emus

384. What do people in Poland traditionally place under the Christmas Eve dinner table?
a) Bread
b) Coins
c) Straw
d) Oranges

385. In Ukraine, what unusual item is traditionally placed on Christmas trees to bring good luck?
a) Garlic
b) Spider webs
c) Salt
d) Coins

386. In Venezuela, what unusual mode of transport do people often use to get to early morning Christmas services?
a) Motorcycles
b) Roller skates
c) Bicycles
d) Scooters

387. In "A Muppet Family Christmas," which Muppet character dresses as Santa Claus?
a) Kermit
b) Fozzie Bear
c) Gonzo
d) Miss Piggy

388. What is the world record for the most Christmas cards sent by an individual?
a) 5,500
b) 62,824
c) 29,000
d) 10,045

389. In what country do people eat a cake called "Rosca de Reyes" on January 6th, Three Kings' Day?
a) Mexico
b) China
c) France
d) Italy

390. In which country is "Oplatki," a Christmas wafer, broken and shared among family members on Christmas Eve?
a) Poland
b) Czech Republic
c) Slovakia
d) Lithuania

391. In which country do people commonly eat "lutefisk" (dried fish) for Christmas dinner?
a) Norway
b) Sweden
c) Iceland
d) Denmark

392. In what country Christmas is celebrated by playing a lottery game called "El Gordo"?
a) Italy
b) Mexico
c) Spain
d) Portugal

393. Which country celebrates Christmas with a tradition called "Joulu Pukki," where a figure similar to Santa Claus delivers gifts?
a) Russia
b) Finland
c) Estonia
d) Latvia

394. In the Philippines, what is the name of the nine-day series of church services before Christmas?
a) Misa de Gallo
b) Pasko Mass
c) Novena Mass
d) Simbang Gabi

395. What is the traditional Christmas drink known as "Glögg" in Scandinavian countries?
a) Hot chocolate
b) Mulled wine
c) Spiced cider
d) Eggnog

396. Who wrote the book "The Polar Express"?
a) Dr. Seuss
b) Chris Van Allsburg
c) J.K. Rowling
d) Roald Dahl

397. What do people in Venezuela traditionally do after their Christmas dinner?
a) Dance the "Gaita"
b) Open gifts
c) Attend church
d) Light fireworks

398. In what country is "Adventskranz," an Advent wreath with candles, a key part of the Christmas tradition?
a) Switzerland
b) Austria
c) Germany
d) All of the above

399. Which Scandinavian country celebrates "Little Christmas Eve" on December 23rd?
a) Finland
b) Norway
c) Denmark
d) Sweden

400. What famous stop-motion TV special features the characters Heat Miser and Snow Miser?
a) The Year Without a Santa Claus
b) Rudolph's Shiny New Year
c) Santa Claus is Comin' to Town
d) Frosty's Winter Wonderland

401. In what country do people burn a figure called "Old Man Gloom" to rid themselves of bad luck on Christmas Eve?

a) Spain

b) Mexico

c) Guatemala

d) Brazil

402. In the book "The Snowman" by Raymond Briggs, what brings the snowman to life?

a) Magic snow

b) A child's wish

c) A scarf

d) The moonlight

403. What is the main character's name in "A Charlie Brown Christmas"?

a) Charlie Brown

b) Snoopy

c) Linus

d) Lucy

404. Which book tells the story of a misfit reindeer who becomes a hero on Christmas Eve?

a) Frosty the Snowman

b) Rudolph the Red-Nosed Reindeer

c) The Night Before Christmas

d) The Nutcracker

405. In "The Nutcracker," what magical land do Clara and the Nutcracker visit?
a) Lappland
b) The North Pole
c) The Land of Sweets
d) Toyland

406. In which country do people practice the custom of "Kallikantzaroi," mythical creatures that come out during the 12 days of Christmas?
a) Greece
b) Turkey
c) Cyprus
d) Italy

407. In the classic TV special "Rudolph the Red-Nosed Reindeer," who is Rudolph's love interest?
a) Clarice
b) Cindy Lou
c) Vixen
d) Donna

408. In "Olive, the Other Reindeer," what animal mistakenly believes she is a reindeer?
a) A dog
b) A cat
c) A rabbit
d) A mouse

409. Who is the author of "The Snowy Day," a classic book often read during Christmas?
a) Ezra Jack Keats
b) Eric Carle
c) Maurice Sendak
d) Shel Silverstein

410. Which Dr. Seuss book features a character who tries to ruin Christmas for the Whos?
a) The Lorax
b) Green Eggs and Ham
c) The Cat in the Hat
d) How the Grinch Stole Christmas

411. In "The Best Christmas Pageant Ever," what is the name of the troublesome family?
a) The Bradleys
b) The McKees
c) The Herdmans
d) The Thompsons

412. Which country celebrates Christmas with "Krampusnacht," where Krampus, a demon-like figure, punishes misbehaving children?
a) Italy
b) Austria
c) Hungary
d) Czech Republic

413. What is the name of the magical train that takes children to the North Pole in "The Polar Express"?
a) The Holiday Train
b) The Christmas Express
c) The Polar Express
d) The North Star Express

414. In "Bear Stays Up for Christmas," what do Bear's friends try to help him do?
a) Decorate his tree
b) Stay awake
c) Write letters to Santa
d) Find gifts

415, Which animal is featured in the Christmas story "The Christmas Cat"?
a) A lion
b) A kitten
c) A tiger
d) A reindeer

416. In "The Velveteen Rabbit," what is the rabbit's Christmas wish?
a) To become real
b) To have friends
c) To meet Santa
d) To be loved

417. What kind of tree does Charlie Brown choose in "A Charlie Brown Christmas"?
a) A tall spruce
b) A pink plastic tree
c) A small, bare tree
d) A golden tree

418. In "The Elf on the Shelf," what is the elf's role during Christmas?
a) To make toys
b) To help Santa with his sleigh
c) To watch over children and report to Santa
d) To deliver presents

419. In "Mr. Willowby's Christmas Tree," why is the tree cut down multiple times?
a) It's too big for Mr. Willowby's house
b) It's too small
c) The animals keep stealing it
d) It keeps falling over

420. What is the world record for the most Christmas carolers singing together?
a) 25,272
b) 15,000
c) 1,500
d) 10,000

421. What is the main character's name in the classic poem "The Night Before Christmas"?
a) Santa Claus
b) The narrator
c) St. Nicholas
d) The reindeer

422. In "The Year of the Perfect Christmas Tree," what does Ruthie's family need to provide for the town's celebration?
a) The Christmas tree
b) The presents
c) The decorations
d) The food

423. In "The Little Drummer Boy," what does the drummer boy offer baby Jesus as a gift?
a) His toy drum
b) His song
c) His blanket
d) A lamb

424. Which Christmas book features a boy who is taken on a magical sleigh ride to the North Pole?
a) The Polar Express
b) The Snowman
c) Santa's Sleigh Ride
d) The Christmas Wish

425. In the story "Santa Mouse," what small animal helps Santa deliver presents?
a) A squirrel
b) A mouse
c) A rabbit
d) A dog

426. In "The Legend of the Poinsettia," what flower becomes associated with Christmas?
a) Poinsettia
b) Rose
c) Tulip
d) Sunflower

427. In "Room for a Little One," what animals are present in the stable when Jesus is born?
a) A dog, a cat, and a bird
b) A cow, a sheep, and a donkey
c) A lion, a tiger, and a bear
d) A horse, a camel, and a sheep

428. In "The Christmas Wish," what does the young girl wish for?
a) To meet Santa
b) To fly with the reindeer
c) To become an elf
d) To help deliver presents

429. In "The Wild Christmas Reindeer," who is tasked with preparing the reindeer for Santa's journey?
a) Teeka
b) Blitzen
c) Clarice
d) Dancer

430. In the story "The Christmas Crocodile," what problem does the crocodile cause in the house?
a) It eats everything
b) It chases the children
c) It knocks over the tree
d) It runs away with the presents

431. What is the name of the boy in "The Polar Express" who doubts Santa's existence?
a) Billy
b) Chris
c) He doesn't have a name
d) Tim

432. Which city holds the record for the most real Christmas trees sold in a single year?
a) New York, USA
b) Oslo, Norway
c) London, UK
d) Berlin, Germany

433. Which holiday, celebrated from December 26 to January 1, honors African heritage and unity?
a) Hanukkah
b) Kwanzaa
c) Diwali
d) Boxing Day

434. What is the Jewish holiday that often coincides with Christmas and lasts for eight days?
a) Passover
b) Rosh Hashanah
c) Hanukkah
d) Purim

435. Which holiday in Mexico reenacts Mary and Joseph's search for a place to stay in Bethlehem?
a) Las Posadas
b) La Navidad
c) Dia de los Muertos
d) Cinco de Mayo

436. What is the name of the holiday celebrated on January 6th, commemorating the visit of the Wise Men to baby Jesus?
a) Epiphany
b) Advent
c) St. Stephen's Day
d) La Tomatina

437. What is the name of the holiday in Ethiopia that celebrates Christmas on January 7th?
a) Enkutatash
b) Timkat
c) Genna
d) Meskel

438. In which country is Boxing Day, celebrated on December 26th, a national holiday?
a) United States
b) Canada
c) Mexico
d) Spain

439. What is the name of the holiday celebrated in Russia and other Orthodox Christian countries on January 7th?
a) Old Christmas
b) Orthodox Christmas
c) Malanka
d) Theophany

440. How many pounds did the world's largest fruitcake weigh?
a) 8,000 pounds
b) 12,000 pounds
c) 6,000 pounds
d) 9,500 pounds

441. In which country do people celebrate "Little Christmas" on January 6th?
a) Ireland
b) Scotland
c) Spain
d) Portugal

442. What is the name of the Finnish tradition where people visit a sauna on Christmas Eve?
a) Julbastu
b) Joulusauna
c) Sauna Night
d) Winter Sauna

443. In which African country is Christmas celebrated by attending church services followed by meals of "injera" and "doro wat"?
a) South Africa
b) Nigeria
c) Kenya
d) Ethiopia

444. Where was the world's largest gathering of people dressed as reindeer?
a) USA
b) Norway
c) UK
d) Australia

445. In Iceland, what is the name of the mischievous holiday characters who visit children in the 13 days leading up to Christmas?
a) Yule Goblins
b) Christmas Trolls
c) Yule Lads
d) Krampus

446. Which country celebrates "Three Kings' Day" (Dia de los Reyes) on January 6th, marking the end of Christmas?
a) Brazil
b) Mexico
c) Italy
d) Portugal

447. In what country do people exchange gifts on New Year's Day instead of Christmas Day?
a) Greece
b) Japan
c) Turkey
d) Egypt

448. What do elves wear on the top of their shoes?
a) snowflakes
b) stars
c) tinsel
d) bells

449. What is the most popular plant given out during the Christmas season?
a) mistletoe
b) poinsettia
c) mint
d) rose

450. What is the famous ballet typically performed during the Christmas season?
a) The Nutcracker
b) Swan Lake
c) Cinderella
d) Sleeping Beauty

451. What is it called when a group of friends draw names and buy a gift anonymously for Christmas?
a) The Santa Claus
b) Pick your Gift
c) Secret Santa
d) Mystery Santa

452. Which Jewish holiday sometimes overlaps with Christmas and is referred to as the Festival of Lights?
a) Yom Kippur
b) Hanukkah
c) Sukkot
d) Purim

453. Who was visited by the angel Gabriel to announce the birth of Jesus?
a) Elizabeth
b) Mary
c) Joseph
d) Anna

454. Where did Mary and Joseph find shelter on the night of Jesus' birth?
a) An inn
b) A stable
c) A cave
d) A house

455. What was the sign the angel gave the shepherds to identify the newborn Jesus?
a) A shining star
b) A baby lying in a manger
c) A golden crown
d) A white dove

456. Who followed a star to find the baby Jesus?
a) Shepherds
b) The Magi (Wise Men)
c) Priests
d) Fishermen

457. What did the angel say to the shepherds when announcing Jesus' birth?
a) "Fear not, for I bring you good tidings of great joy."
b) "A king is born this day in Jerusalem."
c) "Follow the star to Bethlehem."
d) "Rejoice, for the Son of God is born!"

458. What was the name of the king who tried to kill baby Jesus?
a) Herod
b) Saul
c) Solomon
d) Pilate

459. How did Mary and Joseph travel to Bethlehem for the census?
a) By horse
b) By donkey
c) On foot
d) By cart

460. Which gospel in the Bible primarily tells the story of Jesus' birth?
a) Matthew
b) Mark
c) Luke
d) John

461. What song did the angels sing when Jesus was born?
a) "Hark! The Herald Angels Sing"
b) "Gloria in Excelsis Deo"
c) "Silent Night"
d) "O Holy Night"

462. Why did Mary and Joseph travel to Bethlehem before Jesus was born?
a) For a family reunion
b) To escape King Herod
c) To be counted in a Roman census
d) To visit the temple

463. What did the shepherds do after visiting baby Jesus?
a) Spread the word about His birth
b) Returned to their sheep
c) Followed the Wise Men
d) Took gifts to Herod

464. How did the Wise Men know not to return to King Herod after visiting Jesus?
a) They saw a vision in a dream
b) An angel warned them
c) They heard a voice
d) The star disappeared

465. What did King Herod do when he realized the Wise Men didn't return to him?
a) He ordered the death of all baby boys in Bethlehem
b) He traveled to find Jesus himself
c) He declared a feast
d) He forgave the Wise Men

466. Where did Joseph take Mary and Jesus to escape King Herod's decree?
a) Nazareth
b) Jerusalem
c) Egypt
d) Galilee

467. What is the name of the snowman brought to life by a magical hat?
a) Jack Frost
b) Frosty
c) The Snow King
d) Olaf

468. Where was the largest Advent calendar displayed?
a) London, UK
b) Paris, France
c) Munich, Germany
d) Madrid, Spain

469. In the story of "The Nutcracker," who is the villain that leads an army of mice?
a) The Mouse Prince
b) The Nutcracker King
c) The Mouse King
d) The Toy Soldier

470. Who is the ghostly guide that first visits Scrooge in "A Christmas Carol"?
a) The Ghost of Christmas Past
b) Jacob Marley
c) The Ghost of Christmas Yet to Come
d) The Ghost of Christmas Present

471. What is the name of the friendly ghost that appears in "The Nightmare Before Christmas"?
a) Jack Frost
b) Zero
c) Casper
d) Oogie Boogie

472. What is the record for the tallest snowman ever built?
a) 113 feet
b) 85 feet
c) 142 feet
d) 104 feet

473. Which character from "Frozen" is often associated with winter and Christmas due to his icy powers?
a) Kristoff
b) Olaf
c) Sven
d) Elsa

474. Which of Santa's reindeer shares its name with a famous symbol of Valentine's Day?
a) Cupid
b) Prancer
c) Vixen
d) Blitzen

475. Who is the jolly giant that takes Scrooge to see Christmas celebrations in "A Christmas Carol"?
a) The Ghost of Christmas Past
b) The Ghost of Christmas Yet to Come
c) Father Christmas
d) The Ghost of Christmas Present

476. The longest-running Christmas parade is held in which country?
a) USA
b) Canada
c) Finland
d) UK

477. In "Home Alone," what is the name of the main character who is accidentally left behind by his family at Christmas?
a) Kevin
b) Charlie
c) Max
d) Billy

478. Which holiday figure is known for delivering gifts on December 6th in parts of Europe?
a) Santa Claus
b) St. Nicholas
c) Father Christmas
d) Krampus

479. In "Elf," what is the name of the human raised by elves who travels to New York to find his father?
a) Frosty
b) Buddy
c) Jack
d) Kris

480. Which Christmas character is known for leaving coal in the stockings of naughty children?
a) Krampus
b) The Grinch
c) Belsnickel
d) Jack Frost

481. What is the name of the iconic character in "The Nutcracker" who transforms into a prince?
a) The Nutcracker
b) The Toy Soldier
c) Prince Charming
d) The Tin Man

482. Who is the red-suited figure known for flying around the world in a sleigh delivering gifts?
a) Father Christmas
b) Saint Nicholas
c) Santa Claus
d) Kris Kringle

483. Who is the green, grouchy character who tries to ruin Christmas in Dr. Seuss' "How the Grinch Stole Christmas"?
a) Ebenezer Scrooge
b) Oogie Boogie
c) The Grinch
d) Krampus

484. In "A Christmas Carol," which character is known for his miserly and cruel behavior?
a) Jacob Marley
b) Tiny Tim
c) Ebenezer Scrooge
d) Bob Cratchit

485. What is the name of the villainous boogeyman in "The Nightmare Before Christmas"?
a) Oogie Boogie
b) Jack Skellington
c) Dr. Finkelstein
d) The Grinch

486. In "Home Alone," who are the burglars that try to rob Kevin's house?
a) Harry and Marv
b) Vinny and Lou
c) Larry and Moe
d) Ralph and Sam

487. In "Rudolph the Red-Nosed Reindeer," who is the abominable snow creature that frightens everyone?
a) Bumble
b) Yukon Cornelius
c) The Ice King
d) Frosty

488. What is the record for the most Christmas lights on a residential property?
a) 350,000
b) 601,736
c) 412,345
d) 105,300

489. In "The Polar Express," what is the name of the mysterious and somewhat sinister figure who appears on the top of the train?
a) The Conductor
b) The Hobo
c) The Ticket Taker
d) The Engineer

490. In the movie "The Santa Clause," which character attempts to take over Santa's job?
a) Bernard the Elf
b) Jack Frost
c) The Tooth Fairy
d) Scott Calvin

491. In "The Nightmare Before Christmas," which character kidnaps Santa Claus?
a) The Grinch
b) Lock, Shock, and Barrel
c) Oogie Boogie
d) Dr. Finkelstein

492. Which Christmas character in folklore was said to punish naughty children by scaring them?
a) Belsnickel
b) Father Christmas
c) Saint Nicholas
d) Frosty

493. In "Arthur Christmas," who becomes bitter when he is passed over for the position of Santa?
a) Arthur
b) Steve
c) Grandsanta
d) Bryony

494. What is the world record for the largest Christmas tree ever displayed?
a) 72 feet
b) 150 feet
c) 221 feet
d) 110 feet

495. Where was the world's largest Christmas light display, consisting of 1,194,380 LED lights, located?
a) New York, USA
b) Canberra, Australia
c) Tokyo, Japan
d) Paris, France

496. Which evil Christmas figure is known for punishing naughty children by carrying them away in a sack?
a) Black Pete
b) Krampus
c) Belsnickel
d) Jack Frost

497. Which country holds the world record for the largest human Christmas tree?
a) Brazil
b) USA
c) Italy
d) Germany

498. What is the record for the largest Christmas stocking ever made?
a) 1,000 feet long
b) 700 feet long
c) 106 feet long
d) 239 feet long

499. Where was the world's largest gingerbread house built?
a) Germany
b) Texas, USA
c) Sweden
d) Canada

500. What is the world record for the fastest time to decorate a Christmas tree?
a) 24.08 seconds
b) 1 minute
c) 45.2 seconds
d) 32.56 seconds

501. The record for the most Christmas trees
chopped down in 2 minutes is held by whom?
a) Paul Bunyan
b) Jason Wynyard
c) Matt Cogar
d) David Foster

502. Which country celebrates the arrival of Santa
Claus by placing hay and carrots in their shoes for
his horse?
a) Belgium
b) Netherlands
c) Germany
d) Austria

503. In which region of Finland is Santa Claus
Village located?
a) Lapland
b) Helsinki
c) Karelia
d) Åland Islands

504. What special geographical line runs through
Santa Claus Village?
a) Arctic Circle
b) Tropic of Cancer
c) Equator
d) Prime Meridian

505. Which activity is popular for visitors at Santa Claus Village in the winter months?
a) Surfing
b) Dog sledding
c) Rock climbing
d) Sandboarding

506. What is the name of the nearby city that Santa Claus Village is part of?
a) Turku
b) Rovaniemi
c) Tampere
d) Espoo

507. What unique service is offered at the Santa Claus Village post office?
a) Sending letters with a special Santa postmark
b) Free delivery of presents
c) Instant toy-making workshops
d) Reindeer adoption certificates

1. Answer: d) Rudolph
2. Answer: a) North Pole
3. Answer: d) All of the above
4. Answer: b) Helping Santa prepare for Christmas
5. Answer: b) Grass and lichens
6. Answer: a) Building toys
7. Answer: c) Red
8. Answer: c) Sugar cookies
9. Answer: a) Rangifer tarandus
10. Answer: c) Pointy hats
11. Answer: c) North Pole
12. Answer: b) Red
13. Answer: c) Blitzen
14. Answer: a) 2-3 feet
15. Answer: b) Reindeer
16. Answer: a) The elves
17. Answer: b) The Arctic
18. Answer: c) Santa's list
19. Answer: b) Coca-Cola
20. Answer: b) Reading by the fire
21. Answer: a) True
22. Answer: d) Leading the reindeer
23. Answer: c) Cookies and milk
24. Answer: b) She prepares his suit
25. Answer: a) A herd
26. Answer: a) Candy canes
27. Answer: c) Down the chimney
28. Answer: c) 278 feet tall

29. Answer: c) Brown
30. Answer: d) Sleighs
31. Answer: a) Ho Ho Ho!
32. Answer: a) Hot chocolate
33. Answer: d) 3,000 miles
34. Answer: a) Turning invisible
35. Answer: c) Turkey
36. Answer: c) 444 trees
37. Answer: c) Dasher
38. Answer: a) Christmas Eve
39. Answer: a) A big bag
40. Answer: b) A warm scarf
41. Answer: b) 200-300 pounds
42. Answer: d) They drink hot cocoa
43. Answer: a) It can fly
44. Answer: a) Japan
45. Answer: d) 8
46. Answer: c) Pointy shoes with bells
47. Answer: c) He has a magical list
48. Answer: c) Jessica
49. Answer: b) They have thick hooves
50. Answer: d) All of the above
51. Answer: d) Rudolph
52. Answer: d) Tracks Santa's route
53. Answer: b) Caribou
54. Answer: a) Making toys
55. Answer: c) Christmas
56. Answer: b) Silent Night

57. Answer: b) They heat the air before it enters their lungs
58. Answer: a) Go on vacation
59. Answer: c) Sleigh races
60. Answer: a) A toy-making workshop
61. Answer: a) Cupid
62. Answer: d) Forever
63. Answer: c) His elves
64. Answer: d) 1,682
65. Answer: c) Winter
66. Answer: b) Jingle bells
67. Answer: a) Takes a long nap
68. Answer: d) All of the above
69. Answer: c) 50 miles per hour
70. Answer: c) Scout Elf
71. Answer: b) Mrs. Claus
72. Answer: a) A cat
73. Answer: b) Excellent sense of smell
74. Answer: b) Magic snow
75. Answer: d) Black
76. Answer: a) Singing Christmas carols
77. Answer: a) Blue
78. Answer: a) They read letters to Santa
79. Answer: c) He uses magic to create a chimney
80. Answer: d) She decorates Christmas trees
81. Answer: d) All of the above
82. Answer: d) No one knows for sure
83. Answer: b) A Christmas countdown
84. Answer: c) The North Pole

85. Answer: d) All of the above
86. Answer: b) A snowmobile
87. Answer: c) She uses magic to clean it
88. Answer: c) Cold and snowy
89. Answer: a) In the toy factory
90. Answer: b) Rudolph's glowing nose
91. Answer: c) Gingerbread men
92. Answer: b) Arctic Ocean
93. Answer: b) They have to rest in bed
94. Answer: d) Sleigh racing
95. Answer: b) The Night Before Christmas
96. Answer: b) Polar bears
97. Answer: a) Thanksgiving
98. Answer: b) Finland
99. Answer: b) Knitting
100. Answer: a) His elves and reindeer
101. Answer: a) Head Elf
102. Answer: c) He freezes time
103. Answer: b) Pulled by magical reindeer
104. Answer: d) Denmark
105. Answer: c) Christmas Countdown
106. Answer: b) The colorful northern lights
107. Answer: b) Italy
108. Answer: a) USA
109. Answer: a) Make more paper from magic
110. Answer: b) Shakes like a bowl of jelly
111. Answer: b) Santa's sleigh launch
112. Answer: c) Christmas pudding

113. Answer: a) Christmas spirit
114. Answer: c) On the roof
115. Answer: c) Making toys
116. Answer: a) Colombia
117. Answer: c) Cookies and milk
118. Answer: c) Using his magical scroll
119. Answer: a) Rockefeller Center Tree
120. Answer: c) Summer
121. Answer: a) Snowy
122. Answer: c) Aurora Borealis (Northern Lights)
123. Answer: b) The Philippines
124. Answer: a) George Bailey
125. Answer: d) A cozy log cabin
126. Answer: a) Christkindlmarkt
127. Answer: a) Paris
128. Answer: b) 1957
129. Answer: b) He reads letters
130. Answer: d) Winter
131. Answer: c) Sweden
132. Answer: a) Candy
133. Answer: c) Christmas
134. Answer: c) Magical oats
135. Answer: a) Norway
136. Answer: d) All of the above
137. Answer: c) Clip clop
138. Answer: b) Polar bear
139. Answer: a) Mexico
140. Answer: b) Bakken

141. Answer: a) His workshop
142. Answer: b) Baking cookies
143. Answer: d) All of the above
144. Answer: b) $11 million (In Spain, 2019)
145. Answer: b) They pack the presents in the sleigh
146. Answer: d) All of the above
147. Answer: a) France
148. Answer: a) A bell
149. Answer: a) Merry Christmas to all, and to all a good night!
150. Answer: b) They go on training flights
151. Answer: a) Australia
152. Answer: a) Max
153. Answer: d) All of the above
154. Answer: c) Hot Chocolate Party
155. Answer: d) The Netherlands
156. Answer: c) A Christmas Carol
157. Answer: b) Children's letters
158. Answer: a) The North Star
159. Answer: b) Scaring bad children
160. Answer: b) A BB gun
161. Answer: d) All of the above
162. Answer: c) Australia
163. Answer: a) Macy's
164. Answer: c) 18,112 (Derry City, Ireland)
165. Answer: c) Iceland
166. Answer: b) I'm Dreaming of a White Christmas
167. Answer: b) White Christmas
168. Answer: b) 1933

169. Answer: a) By magic mailboxes
170. Answer: a) The Netherlands
171. Answer: a) Jack Skellington
172. Answer: a) A sleigh
173. Answer: b) Colorful dancing lights
174. Answer: a) Spain
175. Answer: c) Claire
176. Answer: b) Deck the Halls
177. Answer: a) All night
178. Answer: d) All of the above
179. Answer: a) Hermey
180. Answer: a) He dances
181. Answer: d) All of the above
182. Answer: c) Coquito
183. Answer: b) A swimming pool
184. Answer: d) India
185. Answer: c) Colorful coats and hats
186. Answer: a) Italy
187. Answer: b) A top hat
188. Answer: a) Santa's sleigh
189. Answer: d) All of the above
190. Answer: a) Poland
191. Answer: b) Michael Caine
192. Answer: d) 1,069 feet
193. Answer: a) By flying with reindeer
194. Answer: a) Mexico
195. Answer: b) Toys
196. Answer: c) Fir

197. Answer: a) Spain

198. Answer: b) Turbo Man

199. Answer: a) Santa Claus Is Coming to Town

200. Answer: a) Making toys

201. Answer: a) Philippines

202. Answer: b) Gift-giving

203. Answer: b) 2003

204. Answer: a) 1957

205. Answer: b) Fried chicken

206. Answer: a) Cameron Diaz and Kate Winslet

207. Answer: a) Franz Gruber

208. Answer: b) Elves

209. Answer: a) Sweden

210. Answer: a) The Santa Clause

211. Answer: b) A drink

212. Answer: a) Lathes

213. Answer: b) Ethiopia

214. Answer: c) White Christmas

215. Answer: a) Tape dispenser

216. Answer: b) 194,672

217. Answer: a) Visit a sauna

218. Answer: b) New York City

219. Answer: b) A diamond ring

220. Answer: c) Fabric

221. Answer: a) Germany

222. Answer: a) The Polar Express

223. Answer: c) Glory to the Newborn King

224. Answer: d) All of the above

225. Answer: a) Italy
226. Answer: b) It's great on spaghetti
227. Answer: b) Elf carts
228. Answer: b) 1984
229. Answer: a) France
230. Answer: a) Bob Cratchit
231. Answer: d) All of the above
232. Answer: a) Spain
233. Answer: a) Poland
234. Answer: a) Edmund Gwenn
235. Answer: a) We Wish You a Merry Christmas
236. Answer: a) Magic wand
237. Answer: a) France
238. Answer: a) Halloween
239. Answer: b) A rock and roll party
240. Answer: c) 2004
241. Answer: a) France
242. Answer: c) The noise
243. Answer: a) Gift-wrapping machine
244. Answer: c) Frasier Fir
245. Answer: c) Norway
246. Answer: a) Screwdriver
247. Answer: d) All of the above
248. Answer: a) A star
249. Answer: a) Canada
250. Answer: b) Naughty/Nice List
251. Answer: a) Quality control checklist
252. Answer: b) Germany

253. Answer: d) All of the above
254. Answer: b) Measuring tape
255. Answer: d) All of the above
256. Answer: d) Multicolored
257. Answer: c) Magic wand
258. Answer: a) 1882
259. Answer: a) O Christmas Tree
260. Answer: b) The birth of Jesus Christ
261. Answer: b) Support
262. Answer: d) All of the above
263. Answer: c) Decorating them with family
264. Answer: a) Mary
265. Answer: c) Bauble
266. Answer: a) Oregon
267. Answer: a) Joseph
268. Answer: c) 1823
269. Answer: a) Pine needles
270. Answer: b) Presents
271. Answer: c) Bethlehem
272. Answer: b) 1990
273. Answer: d) Over 100 feet
274. Answer: a) Water them regularly
275. Answer: b) The day after Thanksgiving
276. Answer: c) Angels
277. Answer: b) Recycling
278. Answer: c) It signifies life and renewal
279. Answer: d) All of the above
280. Answer: b) 1931

281. Answer: d) All of the above

282. Answer: a) Gold, frankincense, and myrrh

283. Answer: d) All of the above

284. Answer: b) 1994

285. Answer: a) Peppermint

286. Answer: c) Whoopie pie

287. Answer: d) Bread

288. Answer: a) Bûche de Noël

289. Answer: d) All of the above

290. Answer: c) Margarita

291. Answer: c) Wassail

292. Answer: b) 1964

293. Answer: d) Candy canes

294. Answer: b) Almonds

295. Answer: c) Christmas Crunch

296. Answer: a) Panforte

297. Answer: a) Glögg

298. Answer: a) Whiskey

299. Answer: d) Coconut

300. Answer: a) Wassail

301. Answer: a) Champurrado

302. Answer: b) 4th century

303. Answer: a) Saturnalia

304. Answer: c) 336 AD

305. Answer: c) Christ's Mass

306. Answer: a) Oliver Cromwell

307. Answer: c) 19th century

308. Answer: c) A Christmas Carol

309. Answer: c) Norse
310. Answer: c) Alabama
311. Answer: c) They banned them
312. Answer: a) Dutch settlers
313. Answer: a) Austria
314. Answer: b) Goose
315. Answer: c) 1840s
316. Answer: d) Christmas Block
317. Answer: a) Queen Victoria
318. Answer: a) Yule
319. Answer: b) The Christmas tree
320. Answer: a) England
321. Answer: b) Christmas pudding
322. Answer: a) Mulled wine
323. Answer: b) Gingerbread cookies
324. Answer: b) A Christmas Story
325. Answer: a) Eggnog
326. Answer: a) Nutmeg
327. Answer: c) Dried fruits
328. Answer: a) Panettone
329. Answer: a) Hot cocoa
330. Answer: a) White chocolate and peppermint
331. Answer: a) Glögg
332. Answer: d) A back scratch
333. Answer: b) Rum
334. Answer: d) Mince pie
335. Answer: a) Raisins
336. Answer: b) Chocolate

337. Answer: c) Chestnuts

338. Answer: c) Glühwein

339. Answer: b) Trifle

340. Answer: c) 364

341. Answer: b) Button

342. Answer: a) Home Alone

343. Answer: b) Rudolph

344. Answer: b) Spain

345. Answer: c) Canada

346. Answer: b) Stollen

347. Answer: b) Norway

348. Answer: b) Père Noël

349. Answer: d) 4

350. Answer: d) All of the above

351. Answer: a) Believe

352. Answer: b) Coal

353. Answer: b) 6

354. Answer: d) Tickle Me Elmo

355. Answer: c) England

356. Answer: c) 1,478

357. Answer: d) Mistletoe

358. Answer: b) The Nutcracker

359. Answer: b) 10 years

360. Answer: b) White

361. Answer: b) "White Christmas"

362. Answer: c) "All I Want for Christmas Is You"

363. Answer: a) Halloween

364. Answer: a) Tinsel

365. Answer: b) Mistletoe
366. Answer: a) Stocking stuffing
367. Answer: a) Yule log
368. Answer: b) A coin
369. Answer: c) United Kingdom
370. Answer: b) To count down the days until Christmas
371. Answer: c) Scrooge McDuck
372. Answer: a) Oregon
373. Answer: c) Finland
374. Answer: b) Yule Book Flood
375. Answer: d) All of the above
376. Answer: b) 151,000 lights (In Belgium)
377. Answer: a) Yule Goat
378. Answer: c) December 26
379. Answer: c) Parol
380. Answer: c) 4,605 items
381. Answer: b) Tió de Nadal
382. Answer: d) All of the above
383. Answer: a) Kangaroos
384. Answer: c) Straw
385. Answer: b) Spider webs
386. Answer: b) Roller skates
387. Answer: b) Fozzie Bear
388. Answer: b) 62,824
389. Answer: a) Mexico
390. Answer: a) Poland
391. Answer: a) Norway
392. Answer: c) Spain

393. Answer: b) Finland
394. Answer: d) Simbang Gabi
395. Answer: b) Mulled wine
396. Answer: b) Chris Van Allsburg
397. Answer: d) Light fireworks
398. Answer: d) All of the above
399. Answer: b) Norway
400. Answer: a) The Year Without a Santa Claus
401. Answer: c) Guatemala
402. Answer: d) The moonlight
403. Answer: a) Charlie Brown
404. Answer: b) Rudolph the Red-Nosed Reindeer
405. Answer: c) The Land of Sweets
406. Answer: a) Greece
407. Answer: a) Clarice
408. Answer: a) A dog
409. Answer: a) Ezra Jack Keats
410. Answer: d) How the Grinch Stole Christmas
411. Answer: c) The Herdmans
412. Answer: b) Austria
413. Answer: c) The Polar Express
414. Answer: b) Stay awake
415. Answer: b) A kitten
416. Answer: a) To become real
417. Answer: c) A small, bare tree
418. Answer: c) To watch over children and report to Santa
419. Answer: a) It's too big for Mr. Willowby's house
420. Answer: a) 25,272 (In the Philippines, 2013)

421. Answer: c) St. Nicholas
422. Answer: a) The Christmas tree
423. Answer: b) His song
424. Answer: a) The Polar Express
425. Answer: b) A mouse
426. Answer: a) Poinsettia
427. Answer: b) A cow, a sheep, and a donkey
428. Answer: d) To help deliver presents
429. Answer: a) Teeka
430. Answer: a) It eats everything
431. Answer: c) He doesn't have a name
432. Answer: d) Berlin, Germany
433. Answer: b) Kwanzaa
434. Answer: c) Hanukkah
435. Answer: a) Las Posadas
436. Answer: a) Epiphany
437. Answer: c) Genna
438. Answer: b) Canada
439. Answer: b) Orthodox Christmas
440. Answer: b) 12,000 pounds
441. Answer: a) Ireland
442. Answer: b) Joulusauna
443. Answer: d) Ethiopia
444. Answer: c) UK
445. Answer: c) Yule Lads
446. Answer: b) Mexico
447. Answer: a) Greece
448. Answer: d) bells

449. Answer: b) poinsettia
450. Answer: a) The Nutcracker
451. Answer: c) Secret Santa
452. Answer: b) Hanukkah
453. Answer: b) Mary
454. Answer: b) A stable
455. Answer: b) A baby lying in a manger
456. Answer: b) The Magi (Wise Men)
457. Answer: a) "Fear not, for I bring you good tidings of great joy."
458. Answer: a) Herod
459. Answer: b) By donkey
460. Answer: c) Luke
461. Answer: b) "Gloria in Excelsis Deo"
462. Answer: c) To be counted in a Roman census
463. Answer: a) Spread the word about His birth
464. Answer: a) They saw a vision in a dream
465. Answer: a) He ordered the death of all baby boys in Bethlehem
466. Answer: c) Egypt
467. Answer: b) Frosty
468. Answer: a) London, UK
469. Answer: c) The Mouse King
470. Answer: b) Jacob Marley
471. Answer: b) Zero
472. Answer: c) 142 feet (In Maine, USA, 2008)
473. Answer: d) Elsa
474. Answer: a) Cupid
475. Answer: d) The Ghost of Christmas Present

476. Answer: a) USA (Peoria, Illinois)

477. Answer: a) Kevin

478. Answer: b) St. Nicholas

479. Answer: b) Buddy

480. Answer: a) Krampus

481. Answer: a) The Nutcracker

482. Answer: c) Santa Claus

483. Answer: c) The Grinch

484. Answer: c) Ebenezer Scrooge

485. Answer: a) Oogie Boogie

486. Answer: a) Harry and Marv

487. Answer: a) Bumble

488. Answer: b) 601,736 (In New York, USA, 2021)

489. Answer: b) The Hobo

490. Answer: b) Jack Frost

491. Answer: b) Lock, Shock, and Barrel

492. Answer: a) Belsnickel

493. Answer: b) Steve

494. Answer: c) 221 feet (A Douglas fir in Seattle, 1950)

495. Answer: b) Canberra, Australia

496. Answer: b) Krampus

497. Answer: a) Brazil

498. Answer: d) 239 feet long

499. Answer: b) Texas, USA

500. Answer: a) 24.08 seconds

501. Answer: b) Jason Wynyard

502. Answer: b) Netherlands

503. Answer: a) Lapland

504. Answer: a) Arctic Circle
505. Answer: b) Dog sledding
506. Answer: b) Rovaniemi
507. Answer: a) Sending letters with a special Santa postmark

THE END

You've made it to the end of this jolly journey through Christmas trivia! Whether you were testing your knowledge, challenging friends, or just soaking in some holiday fun, I hope you had as much joy reading this book as I did creating it.

As we wrap up, may your holidays be filled with laughter, love, and of course, plenty of Christmas cheer. I hope this book has brought a little extra magic to your holiday season!

If you enjoyed this trivia adventure, be sure to check out my other books for more fun-filled facts, quizzes, and challenges. There's always something new to discover, and I'd love for you to join me on the next one.

Until then, stay curious, stay festive, and keep the holiday spirit alive all year long!

Merry Christmas and a Happy New Year!